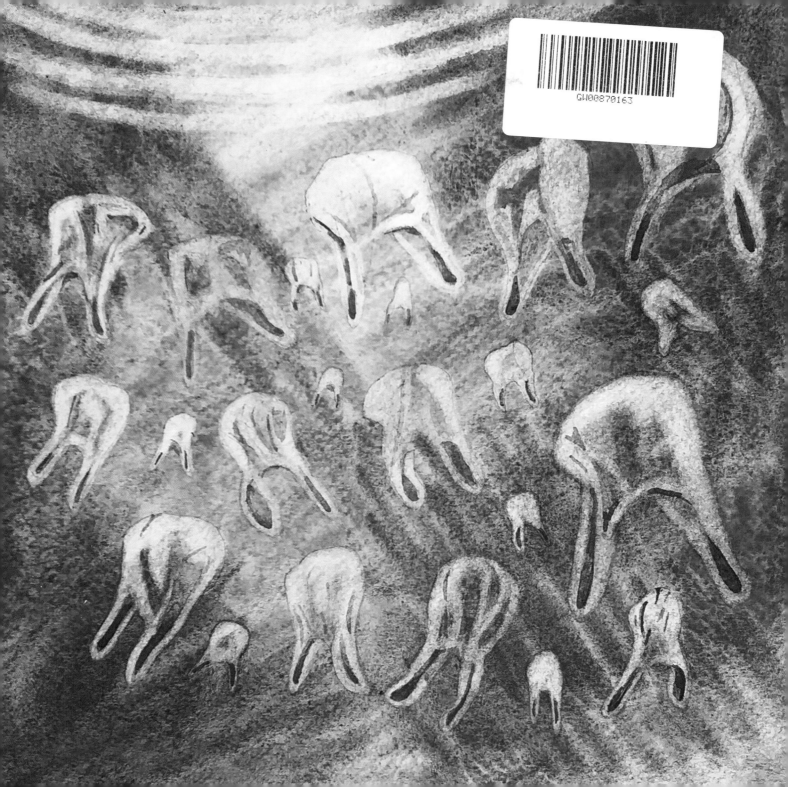

Emily Thuysbaert

Is a dyslexic author. In 2016 she challenged herself to write her first childrens book.

Mia - My Incredible Adventures in Looe

Emily's books are imaginative and creative. She was inspired by her siberian husky to start writing. MIA THE MAGIC HUSKY!

Emily's mission is to help children dream big dreams and to challenge the misconceptions around dyslexia by sharing her story at national events aswell as international.

Emily Thuysbaert © 2019

Books written by Emily Thuysbaert

Mia - My Incredible Adventures in Looe © 2018
Mia - My Incredible Adventures on the Titanic © 2019
Lady the Lady Bug © 2019
Crinkle the Weird Fish © 2019

All illustrations are done by Pat Thuysbaert from © Patsartbox

If you would like to follow or contact Emily Thuysbaert

E-mail: myincredibleadventures@outlook.com
www.facebook.com/myincredibleadventures
Instagram: @MyIncredibleAdventures

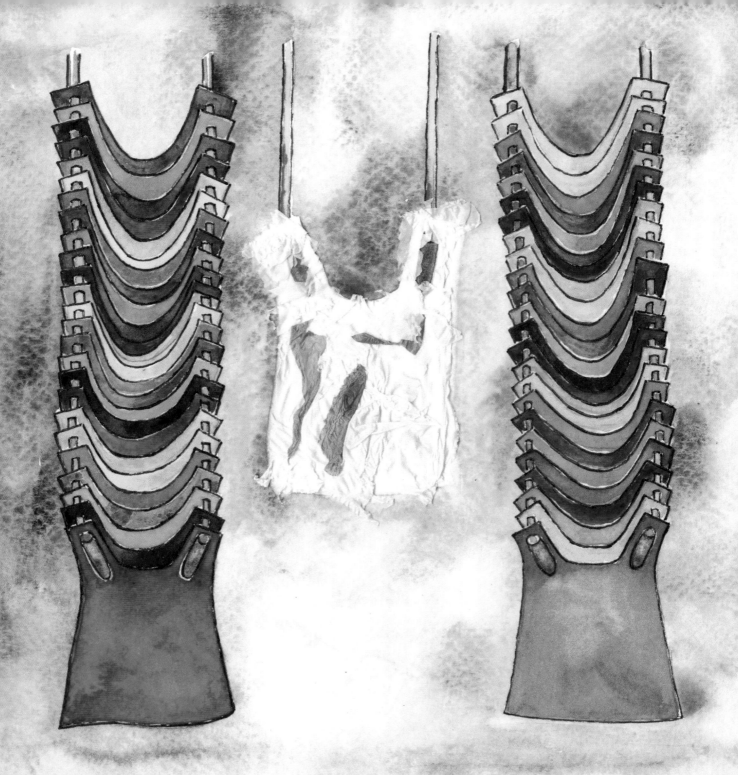

Once there was a plastic carrier bag called **Crinkle**.

He was just like all the other plastic bags
in the world.

Until one day he went on an
adventure;
where he would become known as
Crinkle, the wierd Fish.

Crinkle's adventure start's inside a carrier bag factory where he was made.
He's packed inside a large cardboard box along with hundreds of other plastic carrier bags.

Crinkle over hears people saying "These boxes need to be loaded onto the van going to the supermarket.".

"Ohh what's a supermarket" **Crinkle** thought to himself.

The cardboard box with **crinkle** inside, is wheeled out to the van and loaded onboard.

Crinkle cannot wait to go to this new exciting destination called, 'the supermarket.'

The supermarket was so much more exciting
then **Crinkle** could of imagined.

He learnt that he was going to be used as someone's
shopping bag and he would have a great responsibility
in keeping their shopping safe.

He waited patiently for his turn.
He didn't have to wait long.

Crinkle was excited about the mysterious journey
ahead of him.

He swung happily back and forth in the person's
hand as they walked.

Crinkle knew he was very lucky to be chosen
to go on this adventure.

Crinkle was taken inside the person's home and one by one all of the items he was holding were unpacked. Then put onto the kitchen work top.

Suddenly **Crinkle** was scrunched up into a ball and thrown into the kitchen bin.

He couldn't believe it
"Why am I being thrown away?" he thought.

Searching the sides of his bag for a symbol showing that he could be recycled.

Clear as day there it was!

He was now inside a big black plastic bag with other unwanted items. **Crinkle** is loaded onto a garbage truck and taken away.

After a long, smelly journey the black bag he was in was tipped out.
As it hit the floor, with a thud, the bag split and **Crinkle** toppled out onto a mass of other rubbish.

Looking around in amazement Crinkle saw lots of items with the same recycling symbol as his on their sides.

Crinkle was so upset he cries "We shouldn't be here!!"
Ruffle and Crumple, two carrier bags next to **Crinkle** turn
and say "That's not the worst of it, We will take up to 1000 years to decompose".

Crinkle was still talking to Ruffle and Crumple
when a gust of wind came out of nowhere and
caught **Crinkle**, filled him with air and carries him
up into the sky.
He span and twirled, this way and that.

"Weee." **Crinkle** was enjoying being blown
around but then realised that he was out of control.

"Where will this wind take me?" he thought.

Crinkle was taken far overland. He could see the Ocean coming into view and shouted, "No, No, No" as the wind started to die down.

He landed on top of the water, just as a wave crashed, knocking him under.

As he sank beneath the waves, **Crinkle** couldn't believe the beauty of this new world below. Amazing creatures swam by. They had long arms underneath their bodies.

Crinkle could hear them talk, well whisper. "He looks weird, like a weird fish, I hope no one tries to eat him."

"Eat me?" **Crinkle** repeated. Shocked he realised he looks like a fish and other animals could mistake him for food.

Swimming fast, with his heart pounding hard in his chest. He dodged another creature trying to eat him!

Nexted he escaped an animal that looks like a sword. Swordfish is his name.
Then, a huge creature, went for him. **Crinkle's** told it was a shark.

It had enormous teeth!

Hiding between the rocks and coral at the bottom of the sea, he felt something try to nibble him.

It's a turtle!

STOP!
DO NOT EAT ME!
I AM NOT A FISH!

Crinkle was so sad. He was **C**onstantly hiding and swimming away from the sea creatures.
He had no friends and he felt so lonely.

He floated past other items of rubbish that shouldn't be in the sea.

How did they end up here?" He wondered.

"This isn't the adventure I dreamed of!
All of this rubbish being in the ocean.
We are harming all the sea creatures."
he said in a sad, quiet voice.

North Pacific
Western
Garbage Patch
Eastern
Garbage Patch
North Equatorial

Crinkle was being whisked along in the
sea's current.

Other bits of rubbish were also caught in the current.

Eventually, they all ended up in one huge mass of
rubbish in the middle of one of the ocean's
Garbage Patch's.

Crinkle was horrified.
There, as far as the eye could see, was Garbage.
It must have formed gradually over time.

The currents had gathered up all
the items of rubbish,
just like him,
and here they came to rest.

Crinkle got wedged amongst the mass of rubbish.

As more and more items arrived,
Crinkle realised that soon the sea would
have more plastic rubbish than fish.

He worried that this would stop the sea creatures
that were designed to absorb
the chemical, Carbon, from absorbing it.

During **Crinkle's** time in the ocean he had learnt lots of things. The other day he met some micro-plastics. They told him that they used to be big plastics like bottles and plastic bags just like him.

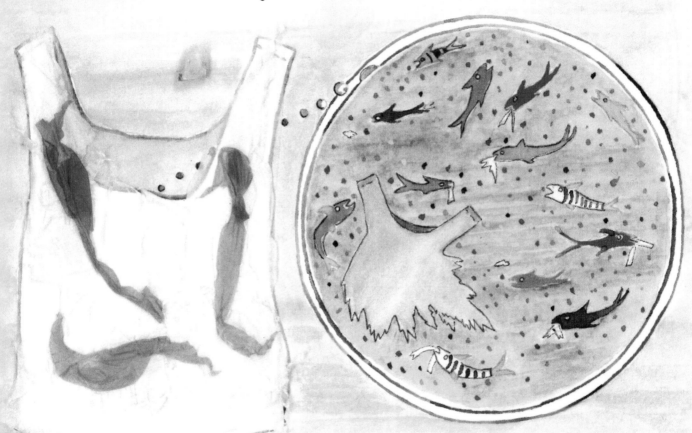

But over time, being in the sea, had caused them to break down. **Crinkle** knew that if he stayed in the ocean he too would become a micro-plastic, and wouldn't be able to stop the fish from eating him.

Crinkle could see that all the horrible plastic and rubbish polluting the ocean would end

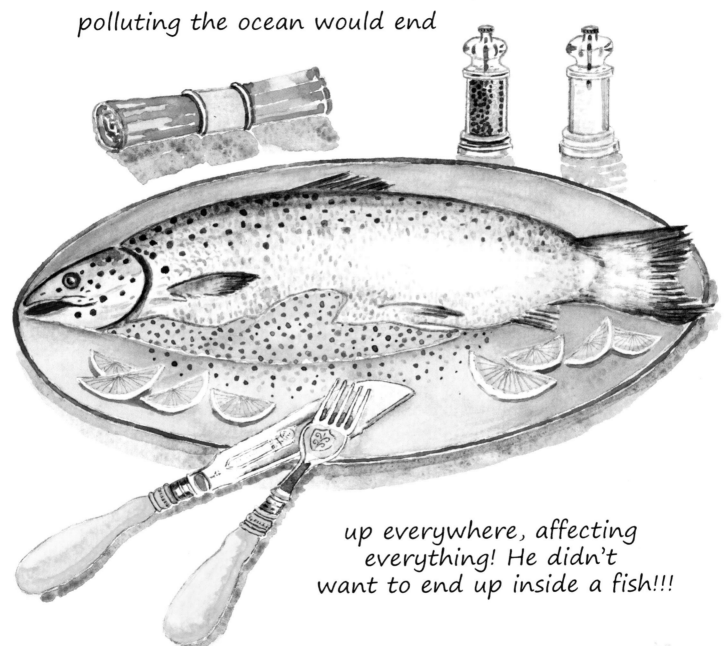

up everywhere, affecting everything! He didn't want to end up inside a fish!!!

An image flashes in **Crinkle's** head he sees a picture of a healthy world verses a sick world.

Driven by what he's seen **Crinkle** swam and swam.

His aim was to get to the seashore in the hope that he would wash up on a beach.

He wants his dream of being recycled to become a reality.

All **Crinkle's** efforts, to get to the seashore, paid off.
Lots of people were on the beach
and **Crinkle** finally got picked up. He was exhausted.

Carried towards a big bag on the beach,
he noticed that there was a recycle
sign on the side of the bag.
He was filled with joy.

Crinkle's dream of being recycled and helping
to not pollute the ocean and the land came true.

Crinkle learnt that when he was recycled, he and
the other items could be made into so many
different things.

Some that could be used to help others! Which is
exactly what he had wanted to do all along.
Be useful.

AMAZING!!!!

Crinkle is the 1st in a collection of books discussing the impacts of climate change on our planet.

Crinkle's story will help children understand that plastic pollution is not just an Ocean issue. It effects our planets climate and is also effecting people's health.

There is a unique aspect to this book I have collected items from a beach clean and these items appear on the pages of **Crinkle** the weird fish!

Can you see them?

@Looeartwork
@myincredibleadventure

e: PatsArtBox@yahoo.co.uk
w: www.PatsArtBox.co.uk
t: +44 (0)1503 262796

Mia Publications

Crinkle *the weird fish © 2019*

Printed in Poland
by Amazon Fulfillment
Poland Sp. z o.o., Wrocław

50945112R00026